Y0-CWR-514

THE WAY THE LIGHT ENTERS

The Way the Light Enters

Lorraine Gane

Black Moss Press
2014

Copyright © 2014 Lorraine Gane

Library and Archives Canada Cataloguing in Publication

Gane, Lorraine, 1953-, author
    The way the light enters / Lorraine Gane.

Poems.
ISBN 978-0-88753-536-9 (pbk.)

    I. Title.

PS8563.A5759W39 2014   C811'.6   C2014-903742-2

Cover image: Marty Gervais
Design & Layout: Jason Rankin
Editor: Vanessa Shields

Published by Black Moss Press at 2450 Byng Road, Windsor, Ontario, N8W 3E8. Canada. Black Moss books are distributed in Canada and the U.S. by Fitzhenry & Whiteside. All orders should be directed there.

    Fitzhenry & Whiteside
    195 Allstate Parkway
    Markham, ON
    L3R 4T8

Black Moss Press

Black Moss would like to acknowledge the generous financial support from both the Canada Council for the Arts and the Ontario Arts Council.

ONTARIO ARTS COUNCIL
CONSEIL DES ARTS DE L'ONTARIO
50 YEARS OF ONTARIO GOVERNMENT SUPPORT OF THE ARTS
50 ANS DE SOUTIEN DU GOUVERNEMENT DE L'ONTARIO AUX ARTS

Canada Council   Conseil des arts
for the Arts   du Canada

CONTENTS

I - Encounter

The Poppies	8
Late Afternoon on the Mountain	9
Early July	10
Swimming Together	11
I Come to the Light in Your Eyes	12
Learning to Love the Rain	13
Crows at Yeo Point	14
Only the Bone	15
December Chronicles	16
The Dancing Firs	20
Wec Na Nec	21
Stratum	22

II - Darkness and Light

Water on Stone	24
The Protestor	25
August	26
On the Bluffs	27
Overnight	28
While the Silence Gathers You	29
Resurrection	30
In the Fields of Iraq	31
Silence the Falling Rain	32
After the Potlach	33
The Secret Language of Slugs	34

III - A Thousand Secrets

Water Songs	36
Solstice	37
Under the Shadow of the Mountain	38
Cedar Grove	39
The Birth of Venus	40
The Raven's Song	41
Lightning-Eyed	42
Frost Flower	43
Soul Catcher	44
Blue Messengers	45
Woman of the Waters	46

IV - Before Dawn

Trilliums	48
The Plum Tree	49
Winter Afternoon	50
The Sacred Well	51
Transparence	52
On the Ferry Back to the Island	53
The Mother Tree	54

V - Hidden Gardens

Autumn Rains	56
The Phantom Orchid	58
The Way Light Enters This World	59
Lunar Eclipse	60
The Beckoning	61

About the Author	62
Acknowledgements	63
Notes	64

I
ENCOUNTER

...every day on the balcony of the sea,
wings open, fire is born and everything is blue again

— Pablo Neruda

THE POPPIES

They slip from hairy buds,
grow pink and red mouths,
thin and crinkled
till the sun irons them
with yellow waves

     This morning
sodden with rain,
they hung their heads
like old women in mourning
while the sun hid in a sullen sky

     Now they frolic in the wind,
bright bonnets open
to the glittering light,
and I think of another day like this
nearly two years ago
so ripe with change

     Early evening,
high on the bluffs over Fulford bay,
your voice opened a door

I stepped through
into the blue trees,
     silence,
the quiet fire of your arms

LATE AFTERNOON ON THE MOUNTAIN

Dark wings erupt
              in a nearby tree,
stillness cracks
as we move into the firs,
your story spawning once again:
a happy childhood, more or less,
the usual teenage antics.
Years later, you shed the city
but it curls
like arbutus skin
over shiny green flesh

My skin peels too
over the bone of loss,
but this is not a lament

I want this dusk falling into firs,
the snap of shoe on the needle path,
the still waters of your eyes,

              beckoning night

EARLY JULY

Sheep by the house

        intent on breakfast,

sky a blue sleeve

           drawing up

a thousand white

        feathers of light

SWIMMING TOGETHER

I marvel at your white skin
for I've never seen you on a hot July day,
blue capping your wide shoulders,
chest curving under dark hair

"Let's go at the count of ten!"
I yell, calling out the numbers to "Blastoff!"

Cold cuts my skin
I look back and you're a young boy
shifting from leg to leg,
swinging his arms for the big plunge

"Come on," I tease like an elder sister,
"Just jump in!"

Several leg shuffles later,
your arms wing out over your head
like a frenzied bird

White streams fly up as you land,
your "YELP!" echoing across the field
where the sheep eye our raucous play

When you emerge,
lips a long "O...it's cold!"
I follow you to shore
crouching in a warm pocket under the fir,
watery light braiding its boughs
and your radiant face

I COME TO THE LIGHT IN YOUR EYES

You open the fridge door and a voice cool as the air asks,
"How did you sleep?" I reply then open the front door,
head down the path to the lake, my heart wrapped tight
in grievances against you.

I slip through the yellow broom, a question rising within:
"Why is it so hard?" Under the pines, the answer comes:
"You make it hard, just love him."

Knots dissolve in my chest, I climb the fence in the field
where the cows lounge in the grass,
eyeing my slow gait to the shore and along the other side
where I disappear into the trees.

Along the trail, my shoes swell in black pools.
Near the house the silence breaks with the sound
of chopping wood, then my name spoken gently.

I come to the light in your eyes —

where I love
          and where I am loved.

LEARNING TO LOVE THE RAIN

Through dark pools across the tent floor
I slip into the cool breath of dawn.
I zip my jacket, tie my hood tight,
then set off into the woods,
my first July 1st on the Coast.
Sheep huddle under a roofed display,
wild roses loosen silky tongues
and I offer my face to the silver wash
quivering on my skin.
Up the hill the cedars close in,
tops a wide umbrella
across the sodden trail.
The forest turns in on itself,
gathering wetness in every root and bough.
Only a bird's wings
clasp through the deepening hush.
I rise quickly into the arbutus trees
then downward to an enclave
of big cedars and firs.
My shoes squeak, my pants darken
above the knees but a soft hissing
calls me farther into the green.
By the time I reach King's Cove
the sea joins the sky
in one continuous shawl of white light.
The rain has nearly stopped —
only the faintest hem of watery veil
touches my face.

CROWS AT YEO POINT

Black wings flash above,
the first warning before high-pitched shrieks
as we approach two arbutus trees
spiraling wildly along the path.
"There must have been something here," you say,
eyeing the wide gap between the trunks
where I step onto hardened earth.
You follow, damp T-shirt around me,
lips cool on my forehead.
Soon more black bodies gather in the trees,
each cry more frenzied than the last.
I want to ignore them,
listen to the swell of waves,
watch the way the light full of flowering
floats through the boughs.
I want to bring back the tethers of my life
from far away places
to this moment on this rocky point,
lip of ocean where shiny heads of seals
slip through dark weeds then disappear
into shadowy blue realms.
Yet the crows will have none of this today,
their voices gathering wrath:
This is our home, you must leave.

ONLY THE BONE

Your eyes, blue notes
           singing

your mouth, boat of joy
           where nothing is lost

when you touch me
I peel back
           skin after skin

there is only the bone of me now
           burning white

DECEMBER CHRONICLES

December 15

This quiet
unbroken under the hiss of cars
thrum of cat at my feet
          holds the immensity
of what is now approaching
like the clouds gathering more
and more of the sky.

The clouds have always known their place
in the larger scheme
and the dark gleaming pond containing the light of those clouds

          reflects beauty we might otherwise not see.

December 16

The sky parts to let through dazzling sun
blinding to my eyes. Light leans into the living room
stroking floor boards with fine dark lines.

The garden, heavy with winter rains, looks almost joyous.
Fields spring up buoyant in lime green, then suddenly,
as quickly as it arrives, the light is gone.

Everything returns to silence — wholly taken in
like a small child embraced in the arms of her mother
over and over until she begins to know herself again.

December 17

In the darkness I'm learning to listen to the silence —
the soft whirring like wind in the trees,
sound of the earth,
turning away from its ancient birth,
                    the slow journey into stone.

What can we know of those times, which have brought us to this
point, billions of people on the earth and still at war with one
another, one-hundred-million people murdered by their own kind
in the last century alone.

                    Yet the light grows.
I sense it in my arms wanting more of the sky, more of the trees,
more of the plants as I gather myself
in the hours of my days.

I see it in the faces of children, newly born and relinquishing
their hold on the other world as they open
fully into ours.

December 18

A sky hardened with grey clouds spills over a ridge of trees
in the yard. The sun, pale and luminescent,
slips into the sky momentarily like a ghost, offering
its fragile light till the clouds fold it back
into their dark wings again.

Let my courage be like a rock, as Rilke says,
holding me firm

                    yet yielding

to the birth of all that is new.

                  The primal fear is death,
which we cannot escape. The unknown breaks open in me,
recalling my human frailty, the great sweep of changes
that will come to this earth, not the massive
destruction cited in the prophecies,
but something much deeper than we can imagine —
the unknown, where all possibilities arise
and for which we have little practice.

Yet nature understands the unknown perfectly.
She breathes it in as part of herself every day,
changing morning to night, clear skies to clouds,
rain into a halo of snow.

December 27

A fog lingers in the harbors, low-lying lakes and fields,
the cars on the roads disappearing in white vapor,
impenetrable except with low beams.
And sometimes the malaise of the world
seems too much to bear — the forests sheared,
oceans spoiled with waste, the soil raped
of nutrients, our farmers going broke
while we continue to believe
that nothing we do will help or worse still,
that this is the course of progress
and science will bail us out as millions
die of AIDS each year and goats are grown
with the DNA of spiders for silky milk.

December 31

After a night of rain, a white mist enfolds the house.
In less than twelve hours the earth will turn over to its new self,
brightened by the glow of fireworks around the world.
The hoopla of the new year.

Still, the wind jostles the slender reeds by the pond,
the sparrows swell in a nearby tree, and I wait, in the silence,
for a glimpse of the distant sun.

THE DANCING FIRS

Boughs loosened by the wind
they sway like women arm in arm
a soft lullaby on this perfect day,
curled leaves at my feet,
the sea calling over the ridge,
stillness deepening as I sit
on the hill alone, wondering
at the gift of these trees
saved from the loggers
thirty years ago
when the land became
the island's largest park
and suddenly I am light,
buoyant, empty as blue air

WEC NA NEC

We're not alone in the dark
among the cedars,

our steps slow to the stones
around a small fir

without boughs or needles,
no crown except a knotted head

faceless and watching our slow breath,
bowed heads, hands cupped in silence.

The spirits move softly among the trees,
like clouds billowing around a full moon.

What can I offer them but a part of myself
— the sound that sings from my bones

into the wide halo of green.

STRATUM

    Dark limbs
        open
    and fall back,
    a heartbeat
    down the long
    roots of trees
    keeping
    what could never
    be lost —
    the soft underbelly
    of silence,
        enfolding light

II
DARKNESS AND LIGHT

Everything here apparently needs us, this fleeting world, which in some strange way keeps calling to us

— Rainer Maria Rilke

WATER ON STONE

On the slopes above the gorge
I hear the hushing in the deep green,
this forest tucked away
beyond the bright light of June,
and down below as we approach the darkened wall
where two white threads unspool into a "V" of rock,
the steady thrum of water on stone
draws me into your arms in cool darkness
as something opens,
a space there all along
but washed clean of the past
and its ash-white bones.
Here in this womb, life is just this:
the cedar folding boughs into the fir,
small fish swimming in the pool by our feet,
the soft husk of our bodies
melding light

THE PROTESTOR
For Bea Neville

She stands before the steel nose of a 40-tonne Mac truck
loaded with sheared and stripped trees

bound for the mill because nothing else will stop
"the butchers who cut and run leaving destruction

in their wake" — not the rallies or phone calls to MPs,
not the countless meetings, letters, faxes or anything

else in the six months since the clear cutting began.
And it seems only right that she should be here

among teachers and carpenters, painters and
rainbow children all the way from Toronto and Montreal,

one-quarter of her 87 years on this afternoon in May,
for somebody has to do something even though

she'd rather be at home making quilts,
her frail body trembling as the young man puts his arms

around her for "protection" till he's dragged off.
When a policeman walks her hand-in-hand

to the white blue-striped car she climbs in and smiles,
her eyes bright under the brim of her Tilly hat

AUGUST

I am not yet empty
           as this morning

ready to hold
every blade of grass, shadow, tree,
                    just for an instant

before it lets them go
into the space

           afternoon becomes

ON THE BLUFFS

Sky, a blue caress
beyond the islands yawning in the sun,
and below mirror-lit waters
where boats pass slowly,
              sails down

Soft lull of the afternoon,
I'm sleeping on a moss-covered mound
while you hurl rocks over the steep edge,
some hitting their mark, most disappearing
soundlessly into still air

I could let myself dream here,
fall into deepness
buoyed by all this light and space,
empty of all desire
till I remember I'm on the edge —
one roll and like the stones
              I'm over into the void

OVERNIGHT

New snow drapes the trees in white lace,
sets top hats on cattails

    Now, sun quivers
in its milky pod,
unfurling through a soft grey sky —

        Tender
awakening of the day

WHILE THE SILENCE GATHERS YOU
For Ellen Haye, 1951-2001

Before the rains began
on the mountain
a deep chill burrowed into my bones,
unnoticed until I returned home

Now, shaking under fleece covers
pulled tight to my chin

I sit indoors watching the dark trees
against the white sky,

the hours too long waiting,
as you are waiting

while the silence gathers you in its soft arms
touching each curve of skin,

weight of bone, long slow muscle
as though it were its own

RESURRECTION

From the door he sees her floating
under white sheets in the tub

and he can think of nothing that will bring her back
from the watery depths in this dream

yet his body knows this ancient place of loss
and cries out "No!" pulling off the veil

shivering with the echo of his voice.
Now etched with silver light,

gashes on her hip, arms, disappear.
Her hair turns red, freckles pool on her skin,

pink hibiscus flowers sprout from her back.
When she opens her eyes, night's ocean enfolds them,

wash of embryonic light

IN THE FIELDS OF IRAQ

No one notices her slip out
from the darkened room where the family
eats noon and night by the fire
and the barefooted girl
wearing only a night shift
walks slowly into the cool air
before the light enters the yard, and thinks
Perhaps I'll find a flower by the water,
so she takes a cup hoping to bring it back full
to the hut where everyone is sleeping.
Nothing stirs outside, not even the dog
whose head lies still in the dust.
She takes the path into the grass
thinking of games she'll play with her brothers
when they awake and sticks she'll collect
with her mother for the first meal,
yet there is something rising in the sky
from the mountains in the west
and now it's louder than thunder.
A rain of heat flashes down
just as she touches a tiny blue flower by her feet.

SILENCE THE FALLING RAIN

The way you look in the morning,
blue bathrobe open to small black curls on your chest,
arms fold me in their familiar weight,
voice deep with the question you ask every day,
my dream unfurls while you grow pensive,
offer a key that unlocks what was lost in the depths.
Sometimes I lose track of where I end and you begin,
a sentence you finish, a thought you act out
as though it were your own instead of my silent wish.
Last night you remembered a line from a book:
The sleeper must awaken from the dream,
tremors through your body into mine.
Now recalling the mist over Fulford bay,
two swans lazing on the afternoon tide as we curve
the shoreline in the car, I think of lives intersecting,
solitudes touching in the black vault we call this universe.
Some say it's the planets aligning
that brings two people together but I know this:
in your arms the stars seem closer, you wash
my darkened face, silence the falling rain.

AFTER THE POTLACH

Where the chiefs would come from Cowichan
and Mayne island and other parts of the coast,
Charlie would not be Charlie any more,
but Chief Charlie of the Salish Sea.
After he'd given away all the blankets
he'd have the right to look them in the eyes
without that longing he'd carried for so many years.
He'd earned money fishing for salmon and cod
in the waters he knew like the back of his hand,
sold fish to C.P.R. boats that came to Beaver Point,
kept the money at the reserve,
but this is not the money they found on Portland Island
when they found his canoe washed up.
They found a hollow cedar shell,
empty of all the dreams he'd taken as his own
through the waters till the waters carried him home

THE SECRET LANGUAGE OF SLUGS

Fat as fingers, their black shiny bodies
grasp some unsuspecting leaf,
innocent stem, ripple of sweet lettuce
they can't resist
as I approach trowel in hand
antennas pulling in, boneless backs curling
before I scoop them into tall grass

Sometimes I put them into the compost,
a colony of dozens in the rhubarb,
but this doesn't bother me,
a slug has to have somewhere to go
and I've got my rules, even if they break them
over and over, slinking back to their favourite spots

I've tried telepathy, but I can't break their code
and now they're breeding
under carrot tops, wilted cabbage and beets.
Soon there'll be hundreds silently conspiring
to take over the garden in the night

III
A THOUSAND SECRETS

At the hour when dreams come true
at the dawn of day
I saw the lips opening
leaf by leaf

— George Seferis

WATER SONGS

1.

They glide on the surface of the pond,
necks high, bodies white against dark water
where sky and green boughs gleam into widening rings.

I stop on the path, the cows come down from the fields,
curious or perhaps wanting to swim like the geese too,
all of us drawn together by some invisible urging.

Now, days later,
I still feel the deepening canopy of green,
the breath of morning on my skin.

2.

Not knowing what I'm looking for
or why I've come,
I follow the path to the mossy knoll above the creek,
stare into muddy waters glinted with sky.
Geese huddle in the grass,
jabbing the ground with yellow beaks,
alders bow to the quiet of morning.

Sometimes I feel like a new creature here,
part of the forest, creek, earth under my feet,
growing moss and wings,
becoming something unknown to myself,
becoming something wild.

SOLSTICE

The sun hangs suspended
bearing its own bright weight

above St. Mary's Lake,
smooth but for tiny waves,

one loon bobbing for fish.
No one has seen me slip

through the overgrown path
and sodden grass to the dock

where I sit on this winter day,
sun touching me everywhere

with dancing particles
that sing all the darkness away,

light and water flowing into my
heavy bones, blood and sunken heart.

I hear the small birds in the reeds,
the leafless willow waiting —

UNDER THE SHADOW OF THE MOUNTAIN

For three days she sits under the cliffs,
emptied of life to find the other life,
then this great loneliness,
the shadow of the mountain,
its strength holding her up.

On the fourth day the she wolf appears
walking quietly in her dreams,
then on the path under the bent tree,
watching her with steely eyes,
hollow of light
as she watches back, not daring to move,
her silence a token of respect,
eyes burning into her breast:

I am the one who calls you,
 listen....

CEDAR GROVE

Before the day opens its bright umbrella
drawing me into its silky fold
I enter the grove of cedars by the creek,
a silence so deep all thought disappears in darkened air
morning waiting to be opened
its loamy aromas of new leaves, flowers,
light weaving golden strands
across the forest floor where my feet
move slowly through saffron cedar seeds.
To know this forest is to know a thousand secrets,
I think, then green lushness
carries me into its silent curves
till I grow resplendent in the dark bodies of trees
where ravens nested for weeks
their raucous cries gone now
in this softness of boughs, parting to let through
the sun's long fingers of light

THE BIRTH OF VENUS

The day we entered the barn
darkness drew us toward the enclosed room.
We stood by the side gate, watched the mother
while her newly born calf searched for teats,
legs wobbly, black head jerking
into the soft underbelly of fur.
The barn was holy that day,
smell of hay, wood, earth mingling
with the mystery of birth,
its imprint on the faces of friends Bob and Diane,
years lifted to reveal
the light they carry in their eyes,
an innocence they belong to, as we all do,
this birth just days after the planet of beauty passed
so close to the earth, the first of two transits
in a hundred-and-twenty years.
Some call this an entry to the new world,
a leap in evolution from which
there is no return.
For months the calf we named Venus
followed her mother through the fields,
feeding at every chance and then some.
She grew wide and sturdy,
sprouted horns on her tufted crown.
Once I tried to feed her dandelions through the fence.
She eyed me suspiciously, stepped forward
then bolted back to her mother's side.
Now she eats apples and vegetable scraps
we throw down by the cedar tree,
accepting this alliance we've entered into,
this co-operation of faith.

THE RAVEN'S SONG

From the time before
when the seas swirled and the rocks heaved
from the belly of the earth
Raven wrestled light from the sun,
fresh water and wind from spirits
guarding what was here.
Raven's song flattened the seas,
raised mountains and trees,
deepened the valleys for rivers.
His song coaxed flowers and ferns from roots,
bears and birds from cedar seeds,
otters and seas from currents running deep,
and from a clam shell on the beach
his song birthed the first human,
wrapping him in seaweed
till he could walk and fish for salmon
and soon there were many
making tools for great cedar poles,
the song keeping them safe, teaching them
to dance and sing and walk quietly in the forest.
When the first ships arrived
some decided not to listen to the song
and its warnings of what might be
and when the sick ones came ashore
there was nothing they could do
but surrender to the sleep,
their bones piling high on the beach.
Still the Raven sang from the highest cedar tree
while the children learned new songs
and the ones who knew wept for what was lost.
Still the Raven sang from the highest cedar tree
till the people began to dance and sing new songs
to all things wild and beautiful.

LIGHTNING-EYED

When he was old enough
Skelechun went to the mountains to seek his medicine
then lightning birds took his eyes,
serpent fire burning everything in sight.
He built a lodge on the highest island peak
where all but his grandmother, now rich,
feared the wrath of his scorching eyes.
Chiefs became his slaves, their daughters his wives,
lugging bear and beaver, salmon and porpoise
up the mountain while he slept and ate.
Then one day two slaves made swords of elk bone,
hid them till Skelechun, eyes downward,
asked them to stoke the fire.
They struck him on the head from behind,
and when he hit the ground, his eyes closing forever,
the chiefs took their daughters and wives home,
the serpents returned to lightning
and Skelechun's home bled into the birth of flowers.

FROST FLOWER

Among dark musky leaves
she calls me down to her white halo,

fine silky threads folding
into her frosted bloom.

I can't resist touching her —
silver pooling on my skin,

but realizing what I've done
I put her back in the leaves

for cool air to keep her intact
a few more hours

while the sun lifts through the trees
and I return home light —

beauty in my eyes

SOUL CATCHER

Bone carved like a whale
to catch the souls of the sick
still has its power,
says the man in the checkered shirt,
his face reminding me of my father's
but not his eyes that hold the gleam
of his grandmother Tuwa'H'Wiye,
daughter of a Cowichan chief.
Found by his father clearing the land,
the bone from the museum
appears in our local paper
and I wonder if it can bring back
the souls here lost to big money now,
land divided and subdivided for homes
over river, rock, earth and tree.

BLUE MESSENGERS

For months I watch them strut up the road
blue veils dragging behind them
bellowing a strange music that reminds me
of blowing on a blade of grass held between two thumbs,
but one day at the mailbox a woman I'd never seen before
tells me "He shot them dead," her face a tight fist,
something wild in her eyes as she strokes her cocker spaniel
then adds, "There were other peacocks up the road
and his went to see them. He's from Alberta, you know."
The next morning pondering the peacocks —
a symbol of the soul, says the book I'm reading —
I pass by the yard of the man from Alberta.
Instead of the blue messengers roaming about the driveway
there stands a shiny black motorcycle covered with a blue tarp.
A sign on the handlebars says: "For Sale."

WOMAN OF THE WATERS
(A myth in four parts)

I
I washed ashore onto land where the trees
bend into the waters.
I could not bear to be alone so I curled around
a great fir, slept under his trunk for forty nights,
my red arms spiraling up to the light

II
As the days passed our roots grew together
in deep silence.
The nights lengthened and the rains
brought winds from the oceans
but his body held me firm even as other trees fell.
In the spring the sun returned, then clear black nights
and tiny birds came to nest and later eagles

III
Under our shadows men and women
made vows of love, children danced
before our entwined presence. We held each other under the
sky's milky roof
until I forgot my ocean roots,
webbed feet, hair of reeds

IV
One day a visitor arrived unlike the others.
Silence grew from his eyes as he knelt before us,
dark hands touching the earth as he spoke a language
I remembered from long ago. The next spring a small tree
appeared on this spot,
lithe and straight with red spiraling arms

IV
BEFORE DAWN

...whatever once I wanted
whatever once I was
is now just

this unguarded light, without
beginning or end

— Margaret Gibson

TRILLIUMS

Eyes still heavy with dreams
and hard-edged thoughts,
I cannot feel the earthy scent
of spring in my bones,
the trilliums I'd touched two days before
hidden in a sea of nettles and ferns.

On the hill I realize I've gone too far,
turn back off the path
where white tongues dusted in gold
hold the light
around a three-fold collar of leaves.

With new-found eyes
a tiny green star appears
at the centre point,
sheer skin rivered in fine lines
growing still as my breath.

Later, among the nettles,
I come upon a secret clutch of flowers,
these ones trilliums too,
their white bodies birthed
into violet hues.

THE PLUM TREE

Such lushness under heavy boughs
bending from the crown,

a green fountain
praising this summer day

while I abandon all caution
in the noonday light

searching among leaves
for the deepest purple orbs

dropping into my hand,
skin tart in my mouth,

pulp watery and sweet,
liquid fire into the rivers of my body

singing all the way
through the stone shell of my heart

WINTER AFTERNOON

My face tips towards yours in such a way
that your breath softens into mine,
your eyelids, cheeks, mouth
lose all they've carried for nearly forty years,
your skin growing almost translucent.
For an instant nothing matters in this face
now a small child's shining
from another life, or one still to come,
or perhaps I'm watching the face
that's been here all along
had I the eyes to see it

THE SACRED WELL

I sense the spirits
before I see Raven in the cedar,
dark and unmoving on a high branch.
It is he I greet before looking down
into the waters, too far below for me to reach.
I climb the stone wall,
inch along the rim of earth
to a trickle over the darkened pool.
Three scoops fill the glass jar,
what remains I sip slowly,
the liquid plush on my tongue.
Into the shadows
I follow a stream downward
where tiny green wings spin above a small pool.
Hummingbird drinks and drinks,
this water as sweet as
the yellow lungs of a thousand flowers.

TRANSPARENCE

This morning
glints of light
in the maple tree —
fallen stars
washing the dark scent
of winter
from my skin

ON THE FERRY BACK TO THE ISLAND

My face pressed to the edge of night,
one light signals from the darkness,
a beacon to the nearness of land
and your arms after weeks away.

In the bay below a pool of light illumines
black waters where seven swans float,
necks high, eyes gleaming
till darkness pulls them in.

Small specks along the shore
grow into bright clusters of yellow,
green, red at Fulford Village,
crowned with fluorescent strings
in the shape of an evergreen tree.

Air cools on my face,
the ferry docks, gate lowers.
Moving slowly with the others
into the carolers
your blue-coated shoulders appear,
ear-to-ear smile that erases
all but the weightlessness of grace.

THE MOTHER TREE

White ribbons lace along
the tips of her arms
skirt flares over fluted trunk
and I standing deep in snow
wait for some glimmer of light
to break through
the steel lid of sky

V
HIDDEN GARDENS

waking in dark the presence of all
the absences we have known

— Phyllis Webb

AUTUMN RAINS

1

In the forest
white caps ignite a dark sea
and as the weeks go by
skins split apart at the edges
torn ragged like flowers,
yet among the sweet decay
a red skull appears
etched with a loosely drawn "Y,"
perhaps for "Yield,"
or maybe "Yes, Yes, Yes!"

2

Darkness,
this room quiet tonight,
my heart still
      in the shudder of rain

3

This morning
a new appearance on the fallen fir —
tongues of translucent gel,
springy to my touch
and Thoreau's words come back to me
from a time before speed was everything:
we must know what we want,
how much is enough?

4

The rains have stopped,
blue sky above the tops of trees
and in this morning light
puff balls spring up in milky pods,
white lace dresses the forest floor,
such growth in the month of death,
underground the earth alive with spores,
and some heaviness lifts,
the song the stream makes
a soft bell that sounds continuously
like all streams drawn towards to the ocean.
Shadows gather the light.
Our lives pass through to the other side
where we cannot reach them,
every breath taking us there.
Slowly.

THE PHANTOM ORCHID

Nothing but these trees
to hold it in darkness,
this white stem
so stark against the sodden bed
of twigs and decaying cedar boughs.
Look how the light grows
in its fluted mouths
singing to the skies in secret tongues
wanting nothing,
not even the cup of my hand
or my admiring eyes
on this day in spring
— the orchid just is —
a narrow reed on the edge
of a fragile world,
its notes carried to places
beyond ordinary listening.
And when the flowers wither
in following days
the sound keeps coming
out of the bells.

THE WAY LIGHT ENTERS THIS WORLD

Dark clouds in every direction
but the island before us arched in rainbow light,
one side of the strait to the other.
From the top deck the light grows into my eyes,
wind hard on our faces
till we move behind glass and steel.

Awe is the salve that will heal our sight,
messages encoded in fern, cedar, sky,
the way light enters this world and is gone
from our eyes yet lingers still,
like those violets, greens, browns, yellows
I see now, six colors in all.

Light passes through a curtain of rain you say,
prisms hold seven colors in their rays,
questions of the heart answered
without knowing the questions,
your face washed in softness
and what grows wide in this light
lives at the apex of our breath as we stand here together,
warmth of your arm against mine,
green shores drawing closer, last sheen of violet fading.

LUNAR ECLIPSE
For Ken

Only a few stars quiver in their silky pods
in the black vault of night
though a thousand galaxies spin
with a thousand million stars beyond our naked eyes
as the shadow of the sun slides across
the moon's lopsided orb,
this meeting of heavenly bodies
a convergence only once every fifty years.
Yet in the parking lot by the car
November air reddens our cheeks,
the earth continues to turn on its invisible axis,
the mountains behind us rest in their black veils
and the geese who wander the surrounding
greens all day sleep hidden in their dark-nested beds.

THE BECKONING

All morning wind lashes the house
as though trying to enter the silence of this room.
Later on the path strewn with boughs
the trees hiss and sigh,
their tall bodies waving in a seesaw of breath.
I know better than to pause here,
black clouds burning orange at the edges,
last licks of sun.
Lamps glow along the driveways by the lake,
reminding me of walks along Toronto's night-lit streets,
wet leaves, November pulling into itself.
Back on the main road, I stop at the crossing,
one light above among translucent blues,
perhaps a plane I think,
till moments later the light grows larger,
streams of reds and blues gleaming from a centre point,
arms shiny knife blades stretching outward.
Cars flash past, lights blind one after the other,
but I cannot move, my head titled to the sky
like a crazed lover, night falling into darkness
around this bright brooch of light.
Look, it seems to say,
The rest of your life is waiting.

ABOUT THE AUTHOR

Lorraine Gane was born in Niagara Falls, Ontario, and grew up in Toronto. In the mid '70s, she graduated from Carleton University's Honours Journalism Program, then worked as a full-time writer and editor for major Canadian newspapers and magazines until 1989, when she began freelancing. In the early '90s, she also started teaching writing at universities and colleges such as Ryerson, McMaster, and Georgian, as well as conducting her own private workshops. Selections from Lorraine's first poetry book, *Even the Slightest Touch Thunders on My Skin* (Black Moss Press, 2002), were shortlisted for the Canadian Literary Awards in 1997 and the League of Canadian Poets chapbook contest. Among her publications since moving to Salt Spring Island, B.C., are three chapbooks (*Earthlight*, *The Phantom Orchid*, and *Beauty and Beyond: Songs of Small Mercies*) and another volume of poems, *The Blue Halo* (Leaf Press, 2014). Lorraine is now working on a memoir and completing a book about writing. She mentors writers through online courses, consultations, workshops, and manuscript editing. www.lorrainegane.com.

ACKNOWLEDGEMENTS

I am deeply grateful to Phil for his love during the writing of these poems.

Special thanks to my mother, Mary, for her generosity and unwavering support. I thank Phyllis Webb for her friendship and gentle mentoring over many years. I wish to acknowledge my dear friends Purna Ma, Cathie Cunningham, Debbie Danbrook, Bernadette Hardaker, and Lee Crawford. Thanks to the Heles for their kindness and beautiful property, Applecroft, where most of these poems were written. I appreciate the love and support of my sisters Judy and Patsy, as well as my brothers Dave, Ken, Richard, and Charlie.

Thanks to Marty Gervais for his vision and Vanessa Shields for her fine editorial help.

A number of these poems were published in the chapbooks *The Phantom Orchid* (Blooming Ground Press, Toronto, 2007) and *Earth Light* (Golden Bough Press, Salt Spring Island, 2001). Thanks to the editors of the following journals, websites and other venues for publishing these poems: "Autumn Rains," *Rocksalt: An Anthology of BC Poets*, Mother Tongue Publishing, 2008; "The Poppies," Monday's Poem, Leaf Press website, 2008; "Winter Afternoon," *Arborealis*, the Ontario Poetry Society, 2008; "In the Fields of Iraq," Poets Against the War website, 2003; "Winter Afternoon" and "The Way the Light Enters This World," exhibited in Through a Glass, Darkly at Artspring performing center, 2008.

NOTES

In "I Come to the Light of Your Eyes" the last two lines are from H.D.'s *Flowering of the Rod*.

"Lightning-Eyed" is based on a legend recounted in *Robert Brown and the Vancouver Exploring Expedition*, edited by John Hayman.

"After the Potlach" is based on the story of Charlie Zalt and his wife, Mary, who lived on Salt Spring Island's native reserve until the 1920s, when their bodies were found washed ashore on nearby Portland Island.

"The Raven Song" is based on a creation story common to First Nations peoples (this version from *Indian Petrogylphs* by Beth Hill) and a story incorporating Haidi Gwaii history, as told by Chief Roy S. Jones Jr.

"The Phantom Orchid" takes its name from one of the rarest flowers in Canada, found only in B.C. at three locations. The plant, which lives off decaying organic matter, can lie dormant for twenty years. Pollution and development are threats to its extinction. The last two lines include fragments from Basho's haiku "The temple bell stops" in *News from the Universe*, edited by Robert Bly, published by Sierra Books.

The Pablo Neruda citation (section I) is from "It is Born," *Fully Empowered*; the quoted lines by Rainer Maria Rilke (section II) are from the *Duino Elegies;* the words by George Seferis (section III) are from "Summer Solstice"; the quoted lines by Margaret Gibson (section IV) are from *Earth Elegy: New and Selected Poems;* Phyllis Webb's lines quoted in section V are from "Non Linear."